Ramadan Activities Guidebook for Kids

Celebrate Ramadan with exciting activities for kids

Mohammed B. Saeed

Table of Content

Introduction

This is the "Ramadan Activities Guidebook for Kids." Welcome. This book is meant to be a colorful and interesting tool for kids to study, investigate, and enjoy the holy month of Ramadan. Islam views Ramadan as a period of intense spiritual contemplation, self-control, and communal bonding. With the help of this booklet, kids can go on an amazing journey to learn about the beauty and customs of Ramadan through a range of entertaining and instructive activities.

Muslims from all over the world gather throughout Ramadan to do acts of prayer, fast from sunrise to sunset, and strengthen their relationship with Allah. Children can learn about their faith during Ramadan, practice qualities like patience and appreciation, and take part in heartfelt rituals with their families and communities. This book offers a variety of engaging and educational activities to help children of all ages experience Ramadan in an approachable and pleasurable manner.

Children will go on a journey of discovery with the help of this guidebook as they investigate the meaning of Ramadan, discover its customs and traditions, create crafts, bake and cook traditional Ramadan foods, play entertaining games and activities, take part in charitable deeds, and think back on the spiritual lessons of the month. Every activity is thoughtfully designed to be entertaining, educational, and age-appropriate, giving kids the chance to learn and develop in a caring and encouraging setting.

Youngsters will learn more about the ideals and concepts that inspire Ramadan, such as empathy, compassion, generosity, and thankfulness, via storytelling, arts and crafts, baking, cooking, and games. Together with building a sense of community and belonging, they will also acquire crucial abilities like creativity, critical thinking, and teamwork.

This guidebook has something to offer every youngster, regardless of whether they are looking to learn more about Ramadan or are fasting for the first time. Children from all backgrounds are invited to participate in the joy and festivities of Ramadan as it is a celebration of diversity, inclusivity, and the richness of Islamic culture.

Let us embrace the spirit of Ramadan with open minds and hearts as we set out on this journey together. May youngsters everywhere find inspiration, knowledge, and happiness in this booklet as they explore the wonders and benefits of Ramadan.

Ramadan Mubarak!

Chapter One

Introduction to Ramadan

Understanding the significance of Ramadan in Islam

Since we were young children, Muslims have understood the significance of Ramadan. Before the days when observing sawm—which is optional until puberty—was expected of us, our parents enlightened us about the customs of our religion and the motivation behind them, which is to become closer to Allah (SWT).

During this season, we must spread the message of Allah (SWT) to young people, regardless of whether we are parents or not. This is similar to what the angel Jibril performed for the Prophet (PBUH) in 610 AD and for the following 23 years. Ramadan customs will endure long after we are gone from this earth because as we pass them on to our children, they will pass them on to their own.

When it comes time for them to properly comprehend the practice, the more likely it is that we teach them early on about the meaning and value of Ramadan and the fast.

For Kids, What Is Ramadan?

The ninth month of the Islamic calendar, Ramadan (also known as Ramazan, Ramzan, Ramadhan, or Ramathan) is observed yearly by Muslims worldwide as a time for fasting, prayer, introspection, and community building. Muslims commemorate the revelation of the Quran, the holy book of Islam, to Prophet Muhammad in 610 AD, which is marked during the sacred month of Ramadan. The Arabic phrase "Laylat Al-Qadar," or "the night of power," refers to this revelation.

The English translation of Ramadan is "burning heat" or "scorching heat," paying homage to the period when it was originally celebrated. Approximately one billion Muslims reside on the planet, and while the Prophet Muhammad (PBUH) and the early Muslims observed Ramadan in hot climates, some Muslims do not.

There is no set date for Ramadan; it is always observed for the full ninth month of the Islamic calendar. This is because the Islamic calendar is based on the lunar cycle, which causes it to change annually (in terms of Gregorian calendar days) by 10 or 11 days.

Tracking the moon

Muslims can follow the moon in three major ways to determine when Ramadan begins:

• The moon hanging above Mecca

Before starting Ramadan, many Muslims wait to see the ninth new moon rise above Mecca. The dates are subject to change without notice due to the unpredictable nature of cloud cover.

• The moon in their neighborhood

Before starting Ramadan, some Muslims would rather wait until they can see the ninth new moon over their neighborhood mosque or in their local area. This may imply that they begin at a different time from individuals who observe the new moon differently; nevertheless, clouds might impede the view, much like Mecca.

• Predictions about astronomy

A few Muslims decide to follow the moon based on lunar forecasts. They now have a more reliable date that is unaffected by inclement weather or cloud cover.

Ramadan Facts for Kids

Not only should you teach kids about the customs of Ramadan, but you should also spend some time explaining some of the month's history, like why the Gregorian calendar never aligns with the dates of the month. Since the Islamic calendar is based on the lunar cycle and Muslims follow their prayer schedules, the month of Ramadan begins around

10 days earlier in the Gregorian calendar each year.

It's also important to explain to kids why some Muslims might not observe sawm because it's rude to question someone who isn't fasting. Among these explanations are:

• Being too elderly or weak to fast safely

• Exempt due to medical reasons (a physician can provide advice)

• If a woman is nursing, pregnant, or menstruation

• Journeying

• Illness or illness

Although it is not necessary for everyone who fits the aforementioned requirements to observe sawm, they are expected to pay Fidya to please Allah (SWT). It is crucial to instill in kids the belief that individuals who choose not to fast during Ramadan are probably still fulfilling their religious duties, as there could be a legitimate cause behind their non-fasting.

The purpose of Ramadan

Muslims seek to deepen their spiritual connections to Allah and their loved ones during the month of Ramadan. They achieve this by refraining from eating and drinking throughout the hours of dawn and dusk every day. Muslims spend their time in prayer, reciting the Quran, and performing charitable deeds throughout Ramadan, which is also a time for unity and introspection. They avoid lying, gossiping, and fighting; instead, they give to charities and spend time with their loved ones.

Teaching the Meaning of the Fast

While it's true that many people recognize Ramadan as a time for fasting from sunrise to sunset, there are additional behaviors that must be avoided during this time, such as lying, gossiping, swearing, and arguing. In addition, Ramadan is a time to practice your Islamic virtues by reciting the Qur'an, praying often, and improving yourself.

Before the first Eid prayers begin, every Muslim is required to pay the obligatory **Zakat al-Fitrana** during Ramadan. Any Muslim, regardless of age, who has more food than they require is allowed to pay. The head of the household should cover the cost of them if the child is unable to pay. Zakat and **Zakat al-Fitr** are not the same thing, even though they are frequently paid at the same time throughout Ramadan.

Sadaqah, the last Ramadan tradition, is when a Muslim performs numerous good deeds without expecting anything in return. Since Ramadan is a time of generosity and selflessness, many people perform sadaqah. Sadaqah can take many forms, such as assisting a stranger crossing the street, working at a soup kitchen, clearing up trash, or lending support to an elderly person.

What occurs if you are not able to fast?
Muslims who are excused from fasting might make up the days they are absent from later in the year. If they are unable to make up the lost days, they will be required to pay Fidya, a daily charitable donation that feeds the hungry and the without. Fidya typically costs less than USD 7 per day, although the cost varies annually based on the cost of basic commodities. For instance, since Fidya is fixed at USD 7, a Muslim who was unable to fast for seven days owing to travel would have to pay USD 7 for each of those seven days, or USD 49, to a Fidya charity.

Marking the end of Ramadan

The completion of Ramadan is celebrated with a unique three-day event called Eid al-Fitr, or the Festival of the Breaking of the Fast. When the new moon first appears in the sky, it starts. Muslims celebrate the end of their fast and give gratitude to Allah on this auspicious occasion.

Muslims visit family members and neighbors on the three days in addition to attending morning prayers. After that, they have a delectable traditional feast with their loved ones. Presents are given to children frequently, and giving to the less fortunate is customary. Ramadan is a time when Muslims from all around the world gather to celebrate their faith as a sign of unification.

Giving a young person an explanation of each of them will be a beneficial way to introduce them to Ramadan and Islam. The Islamic Five Pillars are:

• **Shahada,** or the statement of faith
• **Salat,** or invocation
• **Zakat,** or charitable giving and almsgiving
• **Sawm**, or the month-long fast observed during Ramadan
• **Hajj**, or the journey to Mecca

Ramadan Traditions and Practices

How is Ramadan observed by Muslims? These are five distinct traditions.

The most revered period of the year in Islamic tradition, Muslims celebrate the holy month of Ramadan. Ramadan is celebrated as a month of fasting and prayer around the world. For ages, it has also been associated with a distinct set of customs that capture the unity of the Islamic community.

Here are some of the most beloved Ramadan customs, from the loud cannons that announce the end of the fast to the joyous lantern-lit evenings.

The boom of the iftar cannon

There is a huge celebration marking both the end of the day's fast and the official beginning of Ramadan. At dusk, when the fast is broken, police fire antique cannons to signal the occasion.

The origins of this Ramadan ceremony are the subject of conflicting narratives, although they all point to Cairo. One story goes that a sultan of the Mamluk dynasty in the fifteenth century tested a cannon that was given to him by shooting it at dusk on Ramadan. It's reported that residents of Cairo believed it to be a deliberate iftar ringing.

The sultan commanded that a shell be fired daily at sundown to commemorate iftar after witnessing the public's outpouring of gratitude for the fortuitous move. Up until 1859, live ammunition was utilized; but, due to the large population of the city, blanks were favored. By the end of the 19th century, the custom had made its way from the Levant to Baghdad and finally to the Gulf and North African nations.

. . An early wake-up call

The wake-up call was sounded by a maharani before the invention of the alarm clock. And the custom is still followed. A masaharati's job during Ramadan is to traverse the streets and beat a drum or play a flute to get Muslims up for suhoor, the pre-dawn meal before the fast starts.

Utbah bin Ishaq, an Egyptian administrator in the seventh century, was the first Maserati. He cried out, "Servants of Allah, have suhoor, for there is a blessing in suhoor," as he strolled through the streets of Cairo at night.

Under various titles and tunes, the profession eventually extended to other Islamic nations. To wake people up in Morocco, a gaffer plays a trumpet.

The Maserati in Yemen goes door to door in a community. The function was so well-liked in the Levant that every area had its maharani, or street drummers, who would go around telling the locals to wake up because there is only one true God—Allah the Everlasting.

Lighting the way

Since ancient times, lanterns have been associated with Ramadan, symbolically illuminating the way and welcoming the holy month. Islamic symbols such as the star and crescent moon are also commonly used in décor.

Muslims fast from sunrise to dusk, which drastically alters daily living. However, Ramadan nights are filled with entertainment and a vibrant social scene as people congregate in marketplaces, cafes, and streets decorated with lights and decorations to create a joyous environment for the month.

Every nation has its aesthetic for Ramadan décor. Cairo's streets are embellished with vibrant textiles, lanterns, and lighting. North Africa is dominated by arabesque designs. The ceilings of shopping centers and lampposts throughout the Gulf countries are adorned with colored lights and ornaments featuring crescent moons and eight-pointed stars.

Although there are no official colors for Ramadan, green, yellow, purple, and turquoise—hues that signify serenity and spirituality—are frequently used in décor.

Banquets of plenty...

During Ramadan, the communal meals that are held in most Arab nations might be the greatest example of the Islamic fraternity. One of the most important lessons from fasting is to develop empathy and compassion for less fortunate people.

In Egypt, community gatherings for philanthropic purposes are hosted in residential neighborhoods.

Volunteers work together to provide food, tables, or assistance with the overnight planning of the event.

In Saudi Arabia, the Prophet's Mosque in Medina and the Grand Mosque in Mecca host opulent meals in their courtyards. Mosques and Ramadan tents in the United Arab Emirates have improvised tables with a rainbow of food on them. They are supported by donors and run by nonprofit organizations.

..filled with traditional foods

There are many lavish delicacies on tables that are connected to the holy month. Countries may have similar names for some dishes, but they may have different recipes or components.

Since the Prophet Mohammed broke his fast with dates and water, dates are a mainstay on every table. Muslims have engaged in this activity for centuries. Dates are a great source of energy after a day of fasting since they are high in carbohydrates, fiber, potassium, and magnesium.

To keep the body hydrated and satisfied during the lengthy fast, the majority of Ramadan recipes are stew-like, richer in calories, and less reliant on spices—which may worsen thirst.

The menu for iftar includes dishes like harissa, a rich Moroccan soup with meat, tomatoes, vermicelli, chickpeas, and lentils; three, an Emirati dish of bread cooked in broth with lamb and vegetables;

and molokhia, an Egyptian soup made of molokhia, a green that resembles spinach and is typically served with rice and roasted chicken.

Levantine-style side dishes are popular, such as moutabal and ful (eggplant-based) cooked with fava beans and garlicky lemon oil.

A selection of Ramadan sweets can be enjoyed to round off the meal, such as chakra, a Moroccan cookie flavored with honey and sesame, rice pudding, qatayef, a fried pancake filled with cream or nuts and sweetened with honey or syrup, and Masoud, a Yemeni banana bread pudding.

Chapter Two

Storytime

Special Story Of Ramadan

The Arabic root "ar-ramad," which means searing heat, is whence the name Ramadan originates. Muslims hold that the Quran, the sacred book of Islam, was revealed to Prophet Muhammad when the angel Gabriel visited him in the year 610 A.D. It is thought that during Ramadan, the "Night of Power," or Laylat Al-Qadar, transpired. Muslims observe a fast during that month to remember the Quran's revelation. (See how Muslims are succeeding in America despite being misunderstood.)

The 114 chapters that make up the Quran are believed to contain the exact words of God, also known as Allah. The Quran is complemented by the hadith, which are the companions' reports of the thoughts and deeds of the Prophet Muhammad. Collectively, these comprise the sacred writings of Islam.

3 Key Lessons We Can Learn from the Month of Ramadan

When I was a kid, I used to excitedly await the Azaan, or call to prayer, since it signified that it was time to break our daily fast. We were taught as children that observing the fast throughout the month of Ramadan encourages us to be thankful for the many things in our lives, such as three meals a day, seven days a week, a roof over our heads, clothes on our backs, and so forth. Regardless of our religious beliefs, I've come to understand throughout the years that this month offers a lot more teachings.

Many people have the idea that Ramadan is just about fasting during this month. Many people are likewise surprised to learn that we don't eat or drink anything from sunrise to sunset—not even water.

Not only does fasting help the body get clean and detoxified, but it also helps the mind and soul get clear. It instills in us the values of self-control and patience. It's not easy to fast: you have to get up early in the morning, eat a tiny breakfast before the sun comes up, go about your daily activities, work long hours without your usual caffeine fix, and then wait until the end of the day to break your fast. Whether for professional or personal reasons, we need the qualities of discipline, dedication, and patience in our everyday lives. The main takeaway is that despite the difficulties we encounter, we manage to overcome them and ultimately succeed.

"Truly, ease follows hardship" (The Holy Quran, 94:5).

During the holy month of Ramadan, excellent manners, humility, and generosity are encouraged.

You are urged to show others respect, love, and kindness, to donate to the underprivileged, to have empathy, and most importantly, to be modest and appreciative of your good fortune. Although it is something we ought to do regularly, we frequently forget to do it in our fast-paced society.

Whether for professional or personal reasons, we need the qualities of discipline, dedication, and patience in our everyday lives. The main takeaway is that despite the difficulties we encounter, we manage to overcome them and ultimately succeed.

What is the story behind Eid al Adha?

Eid al-Adha: The Feast of Sacrifice

The Feast of Sacrifice, or Eid al-Adha, is a major holiday observed by Muslims around the world over three to four days. The majority of Muslims will participate in the special prayers that are offered at significant mosques and Islamic centers across the globe, including in the US. Muslims frequently give gifts and dress in new attire. Many people take the day off from work, while children, especially college students, take time off from school. Muhammad, the prophet of Islam, is claimed to have said, "It is a tradition that has come down to us from Abraham," in response to a question on the origins of Eid al-Adha. The historical occurrence when Prophet Abraham was given the order to sacrifice his son Ishmael by God in a dream vision is the source of the Feast of Sacrifice. God sent the angel Gabriel along with a massive ram as he was sacrificing his kid. Gabriel gave Abraham the go-ahead to sacrifice the ram as a ransom for his son, telling him that his dream vision had come true. The narrative appears in Holy Qur'an Chapter #37. Because the Day of Sacrifice is the culmination of the Hajj, or pilgrimage, which is the fifth pillar of Islam, Eid al-Adha holds particular significance. Only men and women who can afford it and are physically capable of making the yearly pilgrimage to Makkah and Madinah in Saudi Arabia are required to do so.

The important lessons from Ramadan

The following is my list of the most important lessons I learned over the month of Ramadan:

• **Balance**

In addition to being patient, we also need to maintain our groundedness. This month, spend some time focusing on your mental and spiritual well-being and removing yourself from the world's materialistic possessions. To stay efficient and preserve a sound work-life equilibrium, you must occasionally disconnect from work and release your tension.

• **Reflection**

We pause throughout this month to consider the previous year. Even while this might be done in a spiritual context, we can apply this to other facets of our lives as well. Spend some time thinking about your routines and objectives (personal and professional). Self-improvement, or knowing where you are and where you want to go, comes from introspection. Finding your good and bad habits will also help you make improvements or changes to them.

• **Creating/Breaking Habits:** Creating a new habit or breaking an old one takes between 21 to 30 days. Ramadan provides us with this chance. One easy example would be to smoke. You are not permitted to smoke during a fast; you would need to abstain from smoking for 30 days. After breaking their fast in the evening, most individuals wind up smoking one or two cigarettes, but if you can avoid cigarettes for the entire day, you can gradually kick the habit. The idea is the same for creating great habits and kicking any bad ones we may have. It is simpler to enhance and modify your behavior if you are committed to doing so and maintain consistency. Maintaining these positive routines for the remainder of the year is the issue.

There are numerous lessons that Ramadan imparts to us that can enhance our lives and character. From having empathy and compassion to forming new routines and always reminding ourselves to keep a healthy balance in our lives.

I pray that everyone will be blessed with good health, prosperity, and happy news during this month of Ramadan. May this inspire you to kick bad habits and pick up new ones?

Kareem Ramadan!

Ramadan Arts and Crafts

However, you don't have to wait for the moon to rise to experience the joy of Eid and Ramadan! These enjoyable kid-friendly Ramadan crafts and activities are perfect to keep or give as gifts to friends!

1. MAGICAL MOON CARD

A Ramadan moon card would be a fitting present during this time of year, as Ramadan commences and concludes with the sighting of the moon!

2. CARD RAMADAN LANTERN

Making a cute lantern card is a terrific way to get your kids excited about making crafts and activities during Ramadan! You should share this with your friends, neighbors, and family because it's quite simple to prepare!

3. BINOCULARS VISITING THE MOON

Since moon sightings determine the start of Ramadan and Eid, why not have some fun and observe how the moon changes phases daily? These adorable moon-sighting binoculars from Hello Holy Days are ideal for the job!

4. DRUMMER DOLL RAMADAN

Before alarm clocks and cellphones, there was a designated Ramadan drummer in many villages. This individual would get up incredibly early in the morning and begin to wander around the streets, pounding a drum, awakening everyone in time for their Sehri. Martha Stewart owns identical village houses and a beautiful drummer doll!

5. EID AND RAMADAN THROW PILLOWS

Among the many kid-friendly Ramadan crafts and activities offered by Hello Holy Days, this throw pillow is a top pick! You can put "Ramadan" on one side of the pillow and "Eid" on the other, switching up the embellishments with sequins and stars.

6. CERAMIC DISH HENNA

In the Middle East and the subcontinent, the henna application is a significant component of the eve of

Eid celebrations. After finishing their tasks, women gather around, take out their cones, and begin creating stunning drawings! These lovely Henna hand dishes are perfect for holding your earrings, cuff links, and more! My Poppet used similar designs on them!

7. CURRENT GEORGE, IT'S RAMADAN!

Little children throughout the world like reading the Curious George books, and this Ramadan version is a relatively recent addition to the series. In this adorably charming tale, George assists his friend Kareem in maintaining his fast. Along with learning about Ramadan, the two also devise strategies for surviving a fasting day! A beautiful book for the younger audience.

8. SUN CATCHERS FOR RAMADAN

Try using these adorable Ramadan sun catchers from Sweet Fajr as inspiration for your home décor in addition to these kid-friendly Ramadan crafts and activities! Use these to give your windows the look of genuine stained glass, or string them up to create a stunning banner that catches the light!

9. TREATS WITH RICE CRISPIES

Who says the crescent shouldn't be on your table but rather remain in the sky? These adorable and delicious-looking crescent and star-shaped rice crispy treats are available at Little Life of Mine. The recipe is really simple; all you need to do is use the appropriate cookie cutters!

10. GOOD DEEDS TREE

These kid-friendly Ramadan crafts and activities are also excellent for promoting virtue. With the help of this adorable tree from Little Wings Creative, kids can record all of their good deeds—such as assisting the neighbor with her bags or serving iftar at the community center—and keep track of them.

11. Ramadan Color by Activity Page Count

This Ramadan color-by-number printable from In The Playroom Blog is perfect for kids and can be downloaded for free. Educating children about the Islamic holy month of Ramadan may be entertaining.

12. DIY Pop-Up Ramadan Card

This month's lunar calendar is aptly illustrated by Picket Fence Arts' charming crescent card. Receiving this card will be as much of a celebration as seeing the crescent!

13. I SNEAK ABOUT RAMADAN EVENTS

Young children have a lot of free time during Ramadan because they frequently don't fast, which might make it difficult to keep them nourished and hydrated! Use this entertaining I Spy printable from Printables Fairy to keep children occupied.

14. RAMADAN BINGO PRINTABLE FOR FREE

After your children have finished playing I Spy, download the Ramadan Bingo printable from Sadeky! After Iftar, this is a terrific idea for a fun family activity while everyone is sleeping.

15. PRESCHOOL CRAFT FOR RAMADAN

This is the noisier version of the Ramadan drummer project that we previously shared on our list of kid-friendly Ramadan crafts and activities! Yas Dunyasi presents an entertaining craft in which the drummer bangs his drum!

16. PRINTABLE RAMADAN PLACEMAT

Since the purpose of Ramadan is to fast for the majority of the day, we should savor the few meals we have! These adorable kids' placemats that can be printed out from the Nurture Store add extra enjoyment to these meals.

17. HENNA HANDPRINT CRAFT SCRATCH ART

Women paint henna to their hands during Eid, and Happy Hooligans' scratchy art hands are a great way to practice during Ramadan!

18. PLAY DOUGH MATS RAMADAN

Printables Fairy has several Ramadan crafts and activities for young children if that's what you're wondering! Toddlers and preschoolers, as well as anybody who wants to play with them, will love these downloadable play dough mats!

19. DIY RAMADAN AND EID JARS: These jars from Jasmine and Marigold are not only one of the simplest ways to make Eid gifts, but they also make lovely pieces of decor for Ramadan! Make a couple in coordinating hues to form a sweet little set!

20. PAPER LANTERN PLACE CARDS FOR RAMADAN

These lantern place cards from Martha Stewart are too adorable for words if you're hosting an Iftar party during Ramadan!

These kid-friendly Ramadan crafts and activities include everything from décor to handcrafted gifts, cards, and even entertaining recipes! Now, quickly head outside and begin searching for the crescent moon!

Remember that Eid comes just after Ramadan, so you'll also need to make and give some Eid projects!

Chapter Three

Cooking and Baking for Ramadan

Now that the holy month of Ramadan has arrived, Muslims everywhere are focusing on fasting and prayer, but every evening, food takes center stage. When both adults and children partake in special delicacies, many of which are frequently created specifically during Ramadan, the iftar is such a special and celebrated time of day.

has been shown to support kids' healthy eating habits and be an effective method of introducing new meals to even the pickiest eaters.

Making Ramadan meals together can be a great way to educate your child on important lessons about the month of Ramadan, such as why we fast and its advantages, in addition to making them feel delighted to be helping their parents in the kitchen. They will look forward to Ramadan every year if this is instilled in them at an early age because they will feel connected.

It could get messy, so be ready, but you two will have a ton of fun!

If your child is fasting, we have compiled a list of iftar and sehri recipes that are nourishing, simple to prepare, and guaranteed to satisfy them from sehri to iftar. It will be messy, so be ready!

10 Recipes for a Child-Friendly Ramadan

1. Date balls

Have a ton of available dates? Process them into a fine powder in a food processor to form date balls. An excellent snack to increase energy and a novel approach to start the day. The possibilities are endless when it comes to coating the date balls with chocolate powder, powdered cornflakes, sprinkles, desiccated coconut, or crushed nuts.

2. No-bake Monster Bars

Is your child trying their hand at fasting this year, or is it their first time? These enormous bars are a fantastic sehri snack or even a post-iftar energy boost. The best aspect is that all of the bars or balls can be prepared in a single bowl with no baking needed, meaning they clean up very easily and are safe! You may switch up what the kids put in the dish by giving them different ingredients like chopped almonds, raisins, dark chocolate chips, M&M Smarties, etc.

3. Juices, Smoothies and Milkshakes

Smoothies, milkshakes, and juices are great ways to provide kids with plenty of fruits and veggies while still being refreshing and quick to open. Using a kid-safe knife and cutting board, assist them in chopping the ingredients before they fill the blender and push the start button. It's quick, simple, and nutritious!

The following combinations are ones you can try:

• Almond milkshake with dates
• Smoothie with strawberries and bananas
• Smoothie with mango and coconut.
• Milkshake with avocado
• Carrot with orange juice
• Pineapple juice and kale
• Milkshake with strawberries

4. Crescent and Star Rice Krispy Treats

Since one of the primary teachings of Islam is to treat others with kindness, involve your children in creating some of these beautiful crescent and star snacks, which they may subsequently give to your neighbors—who are, of course, socially distant. A lesson that tastes like chocolate!

P.S. You can use marshmallow fluff, which is gelatin-free, or purchase halal marshmallows online at Amazon.com.

5. Rolls of pizza

Pizza is always a good choice, especially when it's rolled up like The Kitchn's zucchini pesto pizza rolls. These pizza rolls can sneak in a surprising number of veggies, depending on which veggies you choose to use. They are also freezer-friendly and simple to cook with the kids. Take caution not to consume them all before your child.

6. Overnight Oats

Packed with protein, lipids, and carbohydrates, overnight oats can effectively sustain your child's hunger from sehri to iftar. They can add any fruit they choose to the dish, which is quick and simple to prepare. While there are many recipes available, this is one of our favorites.

7. Dates Covered in Chocolate

Kids love or loathe dates, let's face it, but everyone seems to agree that chocolate-covered dates are the best. Though a little messy, your kids will enjoy dipping, sprinkling, and dunking in various substances of their choice during this activity.

You can top with melted dark, milk, or white chocolate and add toppings like crushed nuts, sprinkles, Oreos, candied fruit peel, rose petals, etc. Children are encouraged to munch on this heavenly fruit because it is semi-healthy.

8. Pastries with Mince Meat

These mincemeat pastries are sure to please both adults and children alike. The smaller children will enjoy rolling and filling the pastry before slathering it with egg wash, but you will need to create the keema filling first and allow it to cool down before involving them. This is a really simple dish that you can teach your older child to make with little to no supervision. You may also use the filling to make spring rolls or samosas.

9. Quesadillas

Similar to pizza, quesadillas are sure to please any number of people. You can pack them full of vegetables or use them as a terrific way to use up leftovers from past iftars. They are ideal for a weekday evening because they are also quite quick to prepare. Before folding it over, your child can help load it high with cheese. They can also help you from a distance while preparing them.

This is a delicious dish for quesadillas with butter chicken.

10. Vegetable and Cheese Muffins

These cheese and vegetable-filled muffins are a great way to pass the time during Ramadan for your kids, and they're also perfect for opening quickly or as a pre-dawn snack. Along with halal turkey bacon and a variety of cheeses, users can add any vegetables they choose, such as chopped broccoli, sweetcorn, onions, mushrooms, and peppers.

Exploring the cultural significance of food during Ramadan

Food has a fundamental role in all cultures. It's a method to express oneself, connect with others, and preserve rich cultural history in addition to being a means of subsistence. Our cultural identity is closely linked to food, which represents our beliefs, history, and tradition.

Intangible Cultural Heritage

Food is regarded as a component of the lifestyle that is carried down through generations as an intangible cultural heritage. Cultural legacy includes essential elements such as traditional culinary methods, dining etiquette, and recipes that can represent the values and beliefs of various groups. Numerous foods and food-related customs and traditions are included in the UNESCO Intangible Cultural Heritage list, such as:

• Al-Mansaf, Jordan's joyous feast

• Tunisian Harissa

• Chinese social customs and traditional methods of processing tea

• Ukrainian borscht cooking culture

• Uzbekistan's Palov culture and traditions

• Arabic coffee: in the UAE, Oman, Qatar, and Saudi Arabia, it is a sign of goodwill.

The preservation of customary cuisine and dining manners depends on educating the next generation about these traditions. Traditional recipes and skills can be taught through culinary lessons and seminars offered by schools and cultural organizations. To ensure that they are passed down to future generations, families can pass down their cooking customs and recipes to their children and grandkids. By promoting traditional foods and ingredients, traditional markets and restaurants can also contribute to the preservation of cultural heritage.

What are the cultural food practices of Muslims?

By Islamic law, all food is deemed halal, or permissible, except pork and its byproducts, animals that have been wrongfully killed or are dead before being killed, animals that have been killed in the name of someone other than Allah (God), carnivorous animals, predatory birds, animals that lack external ears (some birds and reptiles), blood, alcohol, and foods tainted with any of these. Seafood is all halal.

Muslims need to be adept readers of ingredient labels because they are sensitive about what is in their food. Multiple-source food additives, such as gelatin, emulsifiers, and enzymes, need the Muslim consumer to conduct due diligence to verify their legality.

In Muslim-heavy neighborhoods, many Muslims opt to exclusively eat halal-certified food, which can be found in ethnic stores, some ethnic and franchise restaurants, and occasionally mainstream grocery stores. Such certification is offered by the Islamic Food and Nutrition Council of America.

The Holy Book of Islam, the Quran, mentions foods that have significant spiritual significance. The Prophet Muhammad's eating habits provide the model for many modern dining customs. The top foods on the list are olives, honey, yogurt, dates, figs, grapes, pomegranates, and legumes. They appeal to Muslims not just from a religious standpoint but also because they are high in nutrients.

RAMADAN ACTIVITIES AND GAMES

Yes, Ramadan is a great time to spend learning and spending time with your kids. But occasionally, there's a chance to let children engage in enjoyable independent learning and education! Here are a few enjoyable activities that will aid in your kids' education and development while giving you more time to concentrate on your ibadah throughout Ramadan!

• **Exercise: Adding color to verses about fasting**
This is an exercise that kids of all ages can benefit from! One very easy, yet very powerful, approach for parents and teachers to introduce fasting as a cornerstone of Islam is to color in the English translation of the Qur'anic order to fast (Qur'an 2: 183–185). With each written stanza having a

suitable image to go along with it, youngsters learn (and hopefully internalize) the rules and exceptions surrounding fasting.

• **Activity: Sadaqa Jar**

The GiveLight Foundation is an amazing organization that provides global care for young Muslim orphans. GiveLight provides an insightful lesson tying charity (sadaqa) and thankfulness (shukr) in this lovely community post, emphasizing the importance of kids being involved in these important pursuits. For children, creating and keeping a personal "Sadaqa Jar" is a great, useful way to practice the associated acts of kindness and thankfulness.

• **Task: Solving the 99 Names of Allah**

There's no better approach to enhance one's reading comprehension of Arabic and English than to commit Allah's (swt) divine names and qualities to memory. This memory game and flashcard exercise on the "99 Names of Allah" have two advantages. Flashcards that only reflect English words and transliteration can be made for kids who are not familiar with the Arabic alphabet. This way, kids can still learn and, hopefully, retain the 99 names and characteristics of Allah (swt).

• **Video Games for Islamic Studies**

This website is a treasure for Islamic Studies students looking for interactive online games and tutorials! This website is a great resource for kids who are at ease with computers or tablets because it offers a wide variety of materials relevant to Islamic Studies, such as Arabic lessons, stories from the Prophet, nasheeds, and video games. This is especially advised for parents who want to introduce their tech-savvy kids to more spiritually uplifting movies and video games.

• **Task: Making a Ramadan placemat**

Saying the blessing "bismillah" before meals and beverages is a virtue that may be introduced and instilled subtly and creatively with this Ramadan placemat-making project from Karima's Crafts. There are more Islamic worksheets and stencils available on this website that can also be laminated to make placemats! Check out the worksheets that provide unique Ramadan duas related to starting and ending the fast.

• **Qur'an Memorization Starter Kit**

This last task requires a purchase, but we think it's a very worthwhile investment. These carefully designed flashcards and beginning kits for memorizing the Qur'an include surahs in Arabic, and English, and transliterated Arabic for simple recitation. The kits feature sutras, but they also include valuable lessons on subjects like memorizing virtues, teaching children the Qur'an is a great way to give back to society, and how to study the Qur'an.

Ramadan Scavenger Hunt Game -This treasure search game teaches children about the Islamic custom of fasting throughout the month of Ramadan. Students will have the chance to read texts, research topics, and gain knowledge about Ramadan and Eid al-Fitr through this activity. Take a peek at this Ramadan Food Traditions Fact File to pique your interest.

How Are Twinkl Board Games Used?

All of the components needed to play a game (activity board, cards, dice nets, counters, etc.) may be downloaded as PDFs from Twinkl Board Games and printed out quickly! An engaging and successful method for teaching academic subjects to kids while fostering their social, logical, and reasoning abilities. You don't need to worry if your home is devoid of board games because you may print off our selection and engage your kids in enjoyable afternoon activities. Top Board Games for Kids: Knowledge of Emotions The Board Games Pack covers friendship, empathy, and positive affirmations while assisting children in expressing their thoughts. Create your board games with your kids as a fun afternoon activity with this pack of six printable board game templates! The complete set of spring bird board games is available in the

Spring Birds Games Pack! The complete set of board games with a marine animal theme is available in the Sea Animals Board Game Pack! Story spinners, snakes and ladders, and other games are included in the Storytelling Board Games Pack!

Quranic Calligraphy Workshop

Writing passages from the Quran in an artistic and visually appealing way is known as Quranic calligraphy, and it is a highly respected art form. A proficient scribe can walk participants through the fundamentals of calligraphy tools, techniques, and styles in a virtual course on Quranic calligraphy. In addition to appreciating the elegance and profundity of the Quranic text, participants will have the opportunity to practice penning a few verses. This class sheds light on how spirituality and art interact in Islamic culture.

Ramadan Trivia With Aicha Mhamed's Islam Trivia

One of the most enjoyable Ramadan activities is the Ramadan trivia game. In the workplace, using trivia to educate staff members about the significance of Ramadan can be entertaining. Employees can test their religious knowledge and gain a deeper grasp of Islam with the help of Aicha Mohammed's Islam Trivia.

Islam Trivia is appropriate for both adults and children and includes 177 random questions and answers. Employees should, however, voluntarily participate in the trivia. Steer clear of inquiries that seem disrespectful or inconsiderate to staff members.

Chapter Four

Acts of Kindness and Charity

A parent can teach empathy, kindness, and generosity in their child by explaining to them that charity is the act of giving to people in need. Kids can gain insight into the hardships faced by others and comprehend the significance of contributing to the community. A child's feeling of social duty can also be fostered by teaching them about charity. They will discover that even seemingly insignificant deeds of kindness can have a profound impact on someone else's life.

So how, during this unique time of year, can you help your kids grow up to be kind, compassionate adults? Here are four pointers:

1. Establish a connection between philanthropy and Ramadan: Tell your kids that this holy month is both a time for introspection and charitable giving. You may explain to them that Muslims view charitable giving as a means of asking Allah for forgiveness and blessings, and that's why giving to charity during Ramadan is particularly significant.

2. Set a good example: Since kids pick up on conduct from their parents, parents must act charitably throughout Ramadan. You can involve your kids in your altruistic endeavors, like working at a homeless shelter or making food bank donations. This will teach your kids the value of sharing with others.

3. Foster a giving attitude in kids: It's crucial to support kids' innate desire to lend a hand to others. You might ask your kids to select a charity they want to give to and assist them in saving money for their donation. Encourage them to donate their time to a worthy cause as well.

4. Instill gratitude: Lastly, it's critical to instill in your kids an appreciation for what they have. You might clarify that not everyone is as privileged and that we can all contribute to improving the world by donating to others. Encourage your kids to consider what they have to be grateful for and how they may make a difference in the lives of those who might not have as much.

In general, educating kids about charity can help them develop good morals and become kind, responsible adults in the community. Additionally, it can foster in children an understanding of the value of lending a hand to others in need and a sense of thankfulness for what they already have.

Organizing charity drives and fundraising initiatives

Peer-To-Peer Fundraising

Peer-to-peer fundraising is one of the best Ramadan fundraising strategies to draw in more money and boost donations. By using this technique, you can connect with individuals that you might not have been able to contact in the past. It also aids in increasing contributions and attracting new backers. Your friends and relatives are more likely to donate to your fundraising efforts since they are aware of them.

You must motivate your strongest supporters to assist you in meeting your fundraising targets throughout Ramadan. They can accomplish this by interacting with their networks or by using their fundraising pages.

Donation Drive

During the holy month of Ramadan, a contribution drive is a wonderful method for individuals and organizations to support a particular cause or charity. To assist the organization you're supporting in reaching its objectives, you can gather a variety of resources, including food packages, clothing, medical equipment, and other emergency aid. You can complete it online or in person.

Donation drives with a marketing and planning component can be more successful. Another option is to host a drive at your place of employment or a place of worship. By launching an extensive communication campaign, you can connect with potential contributors and prospects and assist those who are experiencing severe poverty.

Ramadan Crafts Fundraiser

One of the most inventive fundraising ideas for Ramadan is the crafts fundraiser, which involves adults as well as children. You can arrange an event for this fundraising where participants can use their creativity to make crafts like lanterns, moon art, or other Islamic artwork that has special meaning for Ramadan.

These handcrafted goods can also be later offered as gifts for charitable causes throughout Ramadan, which will aid fundraisers in raising additional funds for their humanitarian endeavors.

Fundraiser for Spiritual Retreat

Plan a neighborhood get-together to enjoy light fare and talk about the objectives of Ramadan. You can lead a discussion about the goals of the participants and the purpose of your meeting after engaging in a variety of activities that involve reading passages from the Qur'an. To make it simple for individuals to donate to your online campaign, set up a donation box or give them the QR code.

7. Fundraiser for Islamic Lessons

If you or anybody you know can set up a class for students who want to learn more about the holy traditions of Islam while also earning funds for your charity during Ramadan, please do so. It may entail reading passages from the Qur'an, teaching participants the value of almsgiving in Islam, practicing self-discipline, and enrolling in personal development classes. Nothing compares to assisting someone in need and imparting your knowledge. Instead of charging for the class, please consider making a donation that will help someone in need in the future.

Get Started With Your Ramadan Charity Campaign

The fundraising campaign for your charity during Ramadan must be centered on creating possibilities for both donors and recipients. The goal of this month's charity campaign is to increase a believer's subsistence. Islam holds that if you feed someone who is fasting, you will be pardoned and spared from damnation.

Learning and Reflection

We are now in the fortunate month of Ramadan, during which the Qur'an was revealed. We fast during the day and pray at night to commemorate this great event—the revelation of the Qur'an—especially on Laylat al-Qadr, the night the Qur'an was revealed, as Allah informs us:

"We have been sending warnings ever since we sent it down on a Blessed Night."44:3

The benefits of praying and fasting during this month are so great that the Prophet صلى الله عليه وسلم declares: "Anyone who stands for the prayer on

Laylat al-Qadr with sincere faith and hopes for reward will have all of his past sins forgiven. And anyone who fasted during the month of Ramadan will have all of his past sins forgiven."[Agreed Upon] Furthermore, he says, "All of his prior sins will be forgiven to the person who prayed at night during it (Ramadan) out of genuine faith and hoping for reward."[Agreed Upon]

We have been granted three chances to receive forgiveness for all of our transgressions. All spiritual doctors of the heart believe that when the heart is softened by fasting, it becomes more humble and open to the recital of the Qur'an. Maybe this is the wisdom that unites the two most notable acts of worship this month—night prayer and fasting.

It is crucial to remember that during this month, we should not limit our interaction with the Qur'an to the nightly Tarawih prayers; instead, we should dedicate ourselves to studying the Qur'an outside of prayer as well.

According to Ibn 'Abbas' narration, "The most giving person was the Messenger of Allah (صلى الله عليه وسلم), and he would be at his most giving during Ramadan when Jibril would come to him every night and they would study the Qur'an together. The Messenger of Allah (صلى الله عليه وسلم) will undoubtedly be more giving than a passing breeze when he meets Gabriel.[Agreed Upon]

Furthermore, according to al-Bukhari's account from Fatima, during the final year of the Prophet's life, he informed her that, although Jibril and I used to rewrite the Qur'an once a year, this year they changed it twice. I have a sneaking suspicion that this is my moment. And you will be the first member of my family to accompany me.

Our Relationship with the Qur'an

Regretfully, most of us have no connection to the Qur'an at all. The devils have been chained up since we are in Ramadan, the wonderful month of the Qur'an, and now is our chance to rectify the unfortunate situation.

Any debate on the highest quantity of recommended daily reading, whether during or outside of Ramadan, would be strictly academic given the current status of the majority of Muslims. We won't try to read the Qur'an 60 times throughout Ramadan like Imam al-Shafi'i did, or spend the entire night reading the entire Qur'an in one rak'ah like Uthman b. Affan did (yes, it is true; Imam Ahmad and Sa'id B. Jubayr have done it too). I won't bore you with all the tales about how often the Salaf would recite the Qur'an during Ramadan, both during and after prayer (you can probably find them online already, for those who are interested).

Given that the majority of us seldom ever read the Qur'an, to do as they did is well beyond anything we could ever accomplish. On the other hand, I'd like to share this account with you all to think about: Every three days, the Khalifah Walid b. Abd al-Malik would finish reading the entire Qur'an, and he would read it seventeen times during the month of Ramadan. [Refer to Siyar A'lam al-Nubala for his biography.]

The real question is, what can we do to make things right now?

If you are already accustomed to reading the Qur'an during Ramadan, attempt to finish reading it in its entirety if you haven't in the past. Additionally, use this as a chance to start reading the Qur'an every day when Ramadan ends.

If you haven't read the Qur'an during Ramadan before, determine how much time you can devote to reading the Qur'an every day based on your schedule. Avoid overcommitting oneself, since this will just lead to your initial situation of not reading the Qur'an at all.

Keep in mind that "regular deeds, no matter how small, are the most beloved to Allah."[Agreed Upon] As a result, you need to create a realistic Ramadan timetable.

Is There A Minimum One Should Read? What Do the Scholars Have to Say?

Based on a hadith of ~Abdullah b. {Amr in which the Prophet (صلى الله عليه وسلم) directed him to recite the Qur'an in forty days, some scholars, including Imam Ahmad and Ishaq b. Rahuyah disliked a person to not complete the Qur'an at least every 40 days. The minimum is stated in another narration as once every month. It is important to note that this should not be interpreted as a requirement, especially for individuals like new Muslims who are not accustomed to reading the Qur'an or who lack the necessary pronunciation skills.

It would undoubtedly become difficult for them to read the Qur'an at all if they tried to start reading it all at once once a month.

When I brought this up to Sh. Ghassan al-Barqawi suggested that someone study ten verses a day at the very least. He based this on an account of ibn Mas'ud of how the Companions studied the Qur'an verse by verse, 10 at a time.

How Should One Proceed?

This is a great time to try reading and reflecting on the Qur'an since the hunger and thirst that come with fasting soften and make the heart more sensitive. Because of this, I strongly advise studying the Qur'an rather than just reading it. The Prophet's (صلى الله عليه وسلم) Sunnah was to study the Qur'an every night with Jibril. This kind of careful examination of the Qur'an affected the caliber of the Prophet's (صلى الله عليه وسلم) actions. Even though he was already the most giving person alive, this month's study of the Qur'an made him even more so.

Chapter Five

Eid al-Fitr Celebrations

With its name meaning "festival of breaking the fast," Eid al-Fitr signifies the happy conclusion of Ramadan. Muslims use this unique time to rejoice, express gratitude, and spend time with their loved ones.

How is Eid al-Fitr Celebrated

• **Prayers:** Muslims begin the day with unique Eid prayers, which are frequently held in front of sizable crowds outside. We should use this opportunity to thank Allah (God) for all of the support and benefits we got during Ramadan.

• **New clothes:** It's customary to dress in your finest or most recent clothing on Eid as a representation of happiness and fresh starts.

• **Feasts:** Special dishes including sweets, savory dinners, and refreshing drinks are served at feasts that bring families and friends together. A significant aspect of the celebration is eating together and laughing!

• **Gifts:** It's customary for people to exchange gifts, particularly with kids who could get brand-new toys, clothes, or cash.

• **Greetings and visits:** People say "Eid Mubarak!" (Blessed Eid) to one another. Additionally, it's a time to visit friends, family, and neighbors to exchange greetings and build ties within the community.

• **Giving to the less fortunate** before the Eid prayer is Zakat al-Fitr, a charitable donation. This gesture stresses giving to the less fortunate and sharing blessings.

Fun Eid Activities for Kids:

• **Assist in the décor of your house** by creating vibrant decorations, hanging lanterns, and making joyous Eid cards for close ones.

• **Get ready for the feast:** Help out in the kitchen by assisting with kid-friendly duties like arranging fruits or laying the table.

• **Acquire and perform Eid songs:** There are a ton of happy melodies that are full of celebrations and well wishes. For added enjoyment, learn them and sing along!

• **Make your own Eid presents for your loved ones:** Make modest crafts, cards, or drawings.

• **Play games for Eid:** Plan enjoyable get-togethers and games, such as scavenger hunts or classic games, with siblings or friends.

Eid al-Fitr is a joyful time to commemorate the end of Ramadan, give blessings to those you love, and fortify your religion and sense of community. Never forget that the most crucial things in life are to spread joy, be grateful for your blessings, and spend time with loved ones!

Maintaining the Flame: Carrying the Ramadan

Essence Into the Future Beyond the Month: Ramadan is a unique period marked by charitable deeds, prayers, and quality time spent with family and friends. Even though the month is almost over, the wonderful lessons we discovered and the positive habits we developed are things we can carry with us all year long! Here are some ideas for prolonging the Ramadan spirit beyond Eid:

1. Keep up the good deeds:

• **Be compassionate:** Seek out ways to assist those in need, whether it's by lending a classmate a helping hand, making a charitable donation, or just being kind to everyone you come into contact with.

• **Distribute:** Do you still feel the excitement of giving? Keep giving those nearby your toys, snacks, and time. Generosity, no matter how tiny, can have a significant impact.

• **Show good manners:** Keep in mind how important it is to be kind, kind, and supportive. In your daily encounters, carry on the good manners you practiced throughout Ramadan.

2. Continue to Practice Good Habits:

• **Begin each morning with gratitude:** Just like you did during Suhoor, take time to reflect on the blessings in your life.

• **Pray frequently:** Set aside time each day for prayer, even if it's only a quick one right before bed. Do you recall how calm you felt during the prayers of Taraweeh? Consider including quick prayers in your daily practice.

• **Read and learn:** Continue to read passages from the Quran or Islamic tales whenever you get the chance. You may even make reading a daily goal!

. **Stay Connected:**

• Retain close relationships with family and friends: Ask friends over for playdates or make regular trips to see relatives sustain the strong bonds you built throughout Ramadan.

• **Give back to the community** by volunteering at a nearby group or taking part in activities. You and your pals can even plan modest, age-appropriate volunteer endeavors.

• **Share the happiness!** Tell your friends and classmates about the good times and things you discovered during Ramadan. You could even teach them a catchy song for Eid or clarify what Zakat al-Fitr is.

Recall that spreading joy and doing good deeds each day is the key to preserving the spirit of Ramadan. You can share the happiness of Ramadan all year long by carrying on with modest deeds of kindness, moral behavior, and solid relationships!

Bonus Advice: Make a box labeled "Ramadan Memories"! Throughout the month, gather little keepsakes such as decorations, cards for Eid, or photos of memorable occasions. You can go back over these things after Ramadan and remember the happy times.

Conclusion

Best wishes! This concludes your Ramadan Activity Guidebook!

Ramadan has been a voyage of learning, introspection, and family and religious celebration. We hope that this guidebook has inspired you to learn about the lovely customs of Ramadan, participate in enjoyable activities, and experience the joy of compassion and generosity.

Recall that Ramadan is more than just a month of fasting—it's a chance to deepen your relationship with Allah (God), fortify your moral fiber, and give thanks for all of life's benefits.

As you continue after Ramadan, remember these important lessons:

• **Show kindness and compassion:** Make it a point to assist and give to others whenever you can.

• **Act with respect and excellent manners:** Show consideration and kindness to everyone, including those who are not members of your family.

• **Keep up positive behaviors:** Carry on the good habits you formed throughout Ramadan, such as praying every day, reading the Quran, and spending time with loved ones.

• **Talk about your experiences:** Share with your loved ones the things you discovered and went through during Ramadan.

• **Never stop learning and developing:** Throughout the year, keep studying Islam and examining your beliefs.

Above all, keep in mind that even modest deeds of kindness can have a significant impact. Continue bringing the spirit of Ramadan into your everyday life and cherish the happiness of this unique month all year long.

Happy Eid!

We wish you a prosperous and joyous new year that is full of opportunities for growth, learning, and kindness-giving!

Bonus Advice: Remember to keep exploring! Your educational and personal development path is far from over. Ask questions, read more Islamic stories, and learn more about your faith. Keep in mind that maintaining an open heart and a loving spirit are the most crucial things!